Providence and Prayer

by
Fr Francis Selman

All booklets are published thanks to the
generous support of the members of the
Catholic Truth Society

CATHOLIC TRUTH SOCIETY

PUBLISHERS TO THE HOLY SEE

Contents

ISBN 978 1 78469 067 0

Introduction

Perhaps the question most commonly asked by the faithful in parishes is: "Why does God not answer my prayers?" If God does not answer my prayers, we are also likely to ask a further question: "Is there any point in praying? Are not my prayers in vain?" These questions could also be asked by people who do not count themselves as Christians or belong to any church. One source of the temptation to abandon prayer as useless arises from seeing prayer too narrowly as only petition and not realising that prayer, especially silent prayer when we just hold ourselves in the presence of God, perhaps without words, is also something worth doing for its own sake, as it unites us with God and brings us inner peace, a peace that can only come from God. In this pamphlet, however, I shall mainly be concerned with the prayer of petition, that is, praying *for* things.

As there is no use in praying to God for anything unless it is something that comes within his power, the key to answering our opening question lies in understanding a little about providence. What is providence? And how is prayer part of God's plan of providence? A remark in the *Catechism of the Catholic Church* lets us know that there is a close connection between providence and prayer when it says that the prayer of the Psalms is the great school of trust in providence.[1] The plan of this pamphlet will, then, first be to consider providence generally and some main objections to belief in God's providence over all things. Second, to show that asking God for things in prayer rests on belief in his providence and that unanswered prayer still brings us benefits. And, third, to consider miracles, for petitionary prayer implies belief in God's power to work miracles. We shall end by asking what we should ask God for most of all.

What is Providence?

What is providence? Can we even know that the world is ruled by divine providence? After all, so many scientists, physicists and biologists, tell us that the world as we find it has come about by chance. If it is true that human beings with rational life have arisen by chance, we have no reason to think that we are part of a loving providence or that we have an end in life. Providence, however, is an essential part of Christian, and Jewish, faith in God. In his *Commentary on the Apostles' Creed* (article 1), St Thomas Aquinas (1225-1274) wrote:

> "It is well to consider what is meant by this word 'God', for it signifies the governor and provider of all things. To believe there is a God is to believe in one whose government and providence extend to all things, whereas one who believes that all things happen by chance does not believe there is a God."

We may note two points that follow from these words: firstly, St Thomas connects providence with God's omnipotence: he includes providence under belief in "God, the almighty Father, Creator of heaven and earth". Secondly, in order to show that the universe is ruled by divine providence, we need to give some reasons why it is neither due to chance nor to necessity. It is quite common for people who have lost their hold on a true belief about God to resort to belief that our lives are governed by fate. We shall touch on fate in its proper place later. Enough to say here that fate, rightly understood, has a place within providence.

The word 'providence' comes from the Latin word *providere*, which literally means to see before or ahead, and thus to provide for others. That the earth provides so many different kinds of food and fruit for the animals and human beings to sustain their natural life is a sign of God's providence. Many people in ancient times thought that the world was subject to chance, particularly if they were materialists, or that it was ruled by necessity. Some, however, like Socrates (c.470-399 BC), as reported by Xenophon, saw in nature, and especially in the careful design of the human body, signs that the gods had a special love and care for human beings, in other words, that they had a providence for us.[2] Others, like Plato (427-347 BC), were impressed by the order and regular motions of the heavenly bodies and asked themselves whether this came about of itself by chance or was due to wisdom, which comes from a mind. So they either thought, like Plato, it was made by God, although no pagan philosopher could say where the matter came from, or that the world had a soul, as the Stoics held. These were pagans who came to recognise a providential ordering of the world just by reflecting with the natural light of reason on the world without the benefit or aid of divine revelation.

Theologians on providence

The Christian philosopher, Boethius (c.480-524), who is the martyr St Severinus, began his reflections on divine providence, which had a widespread influence on writers in the Middle Ages, by taking up the thought of the ancient pagan philosophers, who saw in the order of the heavens evidence of a wise ruler of the universe. Boethius pointed to the planets and stars as a clear sign of God's ordering of the heavens and hence of his providential rule of the world.

> "Meanwhile there sits on high the Lord of things,
> Who rules and guides the reins of all that's made,
> Their king and lord, their fount and origin."[3]

Boethius was also influenced in his thought by the *Book of Wisdom*: "She [Wisdom] reaches mightily from one end of the earth to the other, and she orders all things well" (*Ws* 8:1). Where the Revised Standard Version translation has "orders all things well", the Latin Vulgate translation that Boethius would have known has "*disponit ominia suaviter*" (disposes all things harmoniously or smoothly). Boethius himself defined providence as "the divine plan (*ratio*), which disposes all things".

St Thomas Aquinas, whose discussion of providence was clearly influenced by the thought of Boethius, added to the definition of Boethius that providence is God's ordering of all things *for an end*: providence is "the plan of the order of things to an end [*in finem*]".[4] St Thomas gives many reasons for holding that the world has an end. Firstly, on the assumption that the world comes from an intelligent Being, for which reasons will be given below, it has an end because intelligent beings act for ends (they can say *why* they do things). Secondly, one cannot order or direct things without giving them an end, just as I cannot give my life a direction unless I have an aim or end in view, such as to reach heaven. Similarly, when I set out on a walk or a journey the direction I take comes from the end that I intend to reach. St Thomas saw that God not only produces things but that he also gives them ends, for which he has made them: for example, trees with leaves to provide shade and birds with wings to fly through the air; insects to devour carrion and so on. If God had produced things but not given them any direction to an end, they would just wander aimlessly and, we may suppose, in vain, so that nature would be frustrated.

Providence and the Creation

The idea of providence, then, goes with that of the world having an end. What is the end of providence? We cannot know this: to know it would be for us to be able to see ahead like God. The end of providence exists solely in the mind of God. All we know is that, as St Paul says, "in everything God works for good with those who love him" (*Rm* 8:28).

The sense of providence has been widely lost by our contemporaries. One cause of this loss is that the progress of natural science over the last two hundred years has led many to think that it will be possible for mankind to dominate the forces of nature. Yet every time that a high wind, hurricane or tsunami strikes, leaving widespread devastation, we should be reminded how comparatively small our power over nature is and is likely to remain so in spite of the technological efficiency that we have so far achieved.

We can see from nature that the world is guided by divine providence, because many things in nature have clearly been made for an end. Plants, for example, reach their completed growth when they produce flowers, which contain the parts by which they reproduce themselves. Likewise, trees reach their end when, after flowering, they produce fruit which contain seeds. Moreover, the various stages of their growth are directed to an end because they occur in the same order, from seed to flower and fruit. Human beings, however, have a higher end than anything in nature, because they also have a rational mind, with which they can know and love their Creator.

The second law of thermodynamics shows us that the world is directed to an end, for it tells us that many processes in nature are irreversible and that the amount of available energy is running down, so that the universe cannot run through perpetual cycles but will come to an end when it reaches a standstill. When one diffuses some ink in a glass of water, one cannot separate the ink from the water: the process of mixing them is irreversible, it runs in one direction.

The Existence and Nature of God

As the universe is moving towards an end, it has been created by an Intelligence, because only minds can conceive the ends for which things act. The way that natural things pursue their ends without having knowledge of their end, as in the growth of plants and animals, declares that they have been given their end by some intelligent Being and so that the world is governed by reason.[5] This is just as when we see an arrow fly towards and hit a target, we know that it has been directed to its end by someone with intelligence and knowledge. The universe has an end because it is neither determined in all its movements (sometimes things fail to act through defects), nor is it purely random or irrational. It is neither the result of necessity nor of chance, because it has been made by free will. Free will always goes with mind and intelligence: one does not exist without the other either in God or human beings. We can tell that the world is a rational one not only because scientists can give us the reasons why things happen in nature but also because the laws of nature can be expressed mathematically.

Mathematics is logical. The Greek word for a reason is *logos*, which is also the Greek word for a word. Thus we read in Scripture that the world was made by the Word, the divine Logos: "In the beginning was the Word, … all things were made through him, and without him was not anything made that was made" (*Jn* 1:1-3). As there is reason in the world, it is governed by divine providence. St Thomas thought that "the certain order of things manifests the government of the world [by providence] as though one were to enter a well ordered house", from which one could tell it had been ordered by someone according to a plan.[6] We can also tell that the world comes from an intelligent Being that has given things their ends in nature, because it is not by chance that things in nature for the most part turn out well or for the best. It is contrary to the idea of things having ends that they have merely come about by chance.

God's goodness

As the cause of the universe lies outside it, for it has been created and brought into existence, so the end of the universe also comes from outside it. This end is the end of providence. The end of everything is its good: it has not been made for a bad end. But nothing created is its own end, because, just as it has received its existence from something before it, so it has received its goodness. Only God is his own good and goodness in itself. He alone does not share in the goodness of anything before him. As things are not their own end, because they are not their own goodness but have received their goodness, so they not just have an end, as a plant is for flowering, but they are also ordered to a good beyond them. Ultimately, all things are ordered to an ultimate end, which is God, who is complete Goodness in himself. If things only had their own end and not an end beyond them, there would be little or no order in the universe. The universe, however, seems to be well ordered. This is especially implied by those who hold that the universe has been finely tuned for producing just the right conditions for the rise of intelligent life in it. The end of things is their good, because God has brought the universe into existence *out of* his goodness, so that he could share his goodness with other beings.

Secondary causes

Providence, then, is the plan existing in the mind of God, by which he directs all things to an end. A plan, however, is pointless unless it is also put into action and executed, just as the point of an architect's plan is for a house to be built. Thus providence has two aspects: we distinguish between the plan in God's mind and the execution of the plan in the course of the world. The plan, in Latin, is called the *ratio* of the order God has given to the world, and the execution of the plan the *gubernatio*, or guiding of the world to its end (*gubernare* literally means to steer a boat: it is the word from which we get the English words to govern and government). While the first, the plan, lies solely in God's mind, God shares the second, the execution of the plan, with other beings. God is the *primary* cause, because he is the cause of everything, but God does not directly cause everything or directly act in everything. It is true that nothing can be a cause except for the power God gives it, but he has made things to be causes on their own. If this were not so but God caused everything by himself, so to speak, there would be little point in the existence of other things, for they would be virtually useless. In directing the world to its end, God uses *secondary* causes: all other beings apart from God are secondary causes. He also uses agents with free will, that is angels and human beings, to execute the plan of his providence. As it says of the good angels, "Are they not all ministering spirits sent forth to serve, for the sake of those who are to obtain salvation?" (*Heb* 1:14) God even uses agents who have little knowledge of him to carry out his designs, as he raised up Cyrus, the king of Persia, to be his instrument in delivering his people, Israel, from captivity in Babylon and leading them back to Jerusalem (*Is* 45:1). God acts in every action of his creatures, for none of them can exist or act unless he holds them in existence. As the *Catechism* says, "It is an inseparable truth of faith in God the Creator: God acts in every action of his creatures".[7] One way, as we shall see in the next section, that God brings about his designs by secondary causes is through our prayers. Also, the *Catechism* adds, through our sufferings, both for ourselves and for the sake of others.[8] Thus God gives us the extra dignity of co-operating with him in carrying out his plan of salvation.

God and the Sparrow

Every single thing in the universe comes within God's providence, because it depends on God for its continued existence. God's providence extends as far as his power, which is to all things, because he holds them in existence every moment. If anything were outside divine providence or escaped the first cause, on which everything else depends for its existence, it would fall back into nothingness. Likewise, cut off from the Creator, we cannot achieve anything. As God's providence covers all things, nothing is too small for God to know and care about it. Not one sparrow falls to the ground without God knowing about it: "not one of them will fall to the ground without your Father's will" (*Mt* 10:29). Or, as Shakespeare says, "there is a special providence about a sparrow".[9] God takes care of all things because he knows all things, including every individual. As the pagan philosopher, Aristotle, remarked, if God did not know the elements (that is, particular things) he would be less wise than we are.[10] God knows all things, because all things are present to him, for he is everywhere. If God takes care of the sparrows, how much more he has concern for each one of us!

Predestination

There is a special part of providence by which God leads beings with free will who are capable of receiving grace to their end, to be with God for eternity. We call this part of providence 'predestination'. There have been two main misunderstandings about predestination. One is that to be predestined is to be determined: in other words our free will has no part to play in reaching our end. The second is a consequence of the first: just as God determines some to be saved, so also those who fail to reach heaven, the damned, are also determined by God to eternal unhappiness and there is nothing they can do in this life to change their lot. Predestination means that no one can be saved without being called and given by God the grace necessary for us to reach our end. This does not mean that he does not require the co-operation of our free response to his grace. God gives the grace for the end which he has chosen us: in the words of St Paul, "He (God) destined us in love to be his sons through Jesus Christ, according to the purpose of his will, to the praise of his glorious grace" (*Ep* 1:5-6). And this plan of God, directing some to eternal salvation, existed "before the foundation of the world". But although no one can be saved without the help of God's grace, if some are lost or 'reprobated', that is not because of anything that God does or has willed but solely due to their free choice, rejecting his grace. God predestines those who reach their blessed end through his grace, but it is a mistake to say that God rejects anyone; rather they freely reject God. We need grace to reach our proper end because it lies beyond and above nature. If we need God's grace, we also need to pray for it. This is just one way in which prayer is part of providence.

Three Difficulties
for Providence

There are three main objections to believing that everything falls within God's providence, so that nothing occurs outside his control:

1. How can evil be part of God's plan, when God only wills what is good?

2. Many things happen by chance and they seem not to be part of God's plan, because a plan is intentional.

3. The world is ruled more by fate than by divine providence, because many events and even human actions seem to be determined.

These are the questions which evil, chance and determinism raise for the belief that divine providence covers all things.

1. Providence and Evil

We distinguish two kinds of evil: physical evil and moral evil. Physical evils are things like tsunamis, earthquakes and floods, which are part of nature. The *Catechism* says that these are part of God's plan because the world is not yet perfect but still in a state of being on the way (*in statu viae*) towards its perfection.[11] St Paul suggests this when he says that "the whole of creation has been groaning in travail until now" (*Rm* 8:22) and speaks in the preceding verses of creation waiting with eager longing for the revealing of the sons of God (v. 19), when it will be set free from its bondage to decay and obtain the glorious liberty of the children of God (v. 21). Physical evils can be for the balance and good of the world as a whole: for example, earthquakes result because they relieve pressure beneath the surface of the Earth.

The second kind of evil is moral evil: this is the evil that agents with free will, fallen angels and human beings, *do* rather than suffer. God does not will moral evil but it is part of his plan of providence because he permits it. We should note that some evils which might be counted as physical evils are the result of human free will and sin. For example, many people suffer illness and disease without being responsible for them, but illness and disease, which lead to death, entered the world through the Fall: "Sin came into the world through one man and death through sin" (*Rm* 5:12). The droughts of recent decades in South America are the result of free human agency through the deforestation of great areas.

Explanations for evil

There is no contradiction in holding that God's providential rule of the world includes evil for two reasons. First, providence includes free will. Second, God can draw good out of evil and thus turn it to his own end. God does not will the evils that come from the injustice of men but they come within providence, because it was part of God's plan to create beings with free will. As St Thomas Aquinas says, it is better that some beings in the universe have free will rather than nothing or no one created has any understanding of his or her actions. As Cardinal Schönborn remarks, God has given us freedom because he created us in freedom.[12] If beings truly have free will, it is always possible that some of them will voluntarily turn away from God. But it is better that we have free will, although there is this possibility of turning away from God, because free will is part of what constitutes our human dignity, which sets us above all the animals. God permits evil, so that it comes within his plan, because he respects our liberty. It is a sign of greater strength in a ruler to permit opposition and still retain control than to prevent all possibility of breaking the laws by taking away the freedom of the citizens, just as parents give their children freedom and sometimes allow them to do something which they know will not turn out well. Once creatures choose to oppose God and do evil, however, God is not thwarted or frustrated in his plan of providence because he can use evil for his own good ends.

God shows his almighty power not by preventing or stopping evil but by drawing good out of it. There is no evil that God permits and he cannot draw good out of it, because he is all powerful.[13] If all evils were prevented, St Thomas says, many good things would also be missed.[14] For example, the evil of persecution by dictators has brought forth the example of the courage and patience of martyrs and led them to win the crown of glory. Generally, trials and suffering are also the occasions that produce virtues in us that we might not otherwise have acquired and shown. The evil that Joseph's brothers willed to him by leaving him in a pit worked to his and their good because, as a result, Joseph rose to become a powerful minister in Egypt and so be able to help his brothers when they came to him in their time of famine (*Gn* 45:8, 50:20). From the Fall has come the redemption and grace of Christ.

The evil of suffering an illness or misfortune has often led to a conversion, as happened when St Ignatius of Loyola, when recovering from an injury to his leg in defending the city of Pamplona against a siege, began to turn his thoughts more to Christ and resolved to follow him wholly. Boethius observed that good fortune often deceives us but bad fortune brings us back to our true good.[15]

2. Providence and Chance

Many things in the world apparently happen by chance (which is not at all the same thing as to say that the world or universe is due to chance). This poses two problems for belief in divine providence. First, things that happen by chance do not occur according to a plan. Second, the plan of divine providence is certain and cannot fail to reach the end God has in mind, so things that happen by chance must fall outside his providence or have no place in providence. How then is chance compatible with providence? Providence is infallible, that is God's plan for it will not fail to reach its end, because God knows and sees all things, so nothing occurs with which he had not reckoned. And he is all-powerful, so he has the power to bring his plan to the conclusion he has intended from eternity and cannot ultimately be frustrated by the opposition of those who do evil. Although God will certainly bring his plan to its end, nonetheless chance has a place in it.

The first meetings of many people occur by chance, yet we often rightly regard them as 'providential', because in this way people who marry one another or become friends have first met, or the meeting marks a decisive new turn in the life of at least one of them. So this is something that happens by chance but seems to be part of a wider plan. Chance can be part of a plan. For example, it seems to be by chance that the seeds of sycamore trees are carried through the air aimlessly and thus scattered but it is part of the plan of nature that this should be the way that sycamore trees get their seeds sown in the ground. Aristotle remarked that nothing is accidental without being accidental *to* something else and so that chance events are part of a framework, which itself has some purpose.[16] In other words, you do not get chance by itself without purpose in the world. A nice example of events in people's lives appearing to be by chance but being part of a larger plan is provided by Thornton Wilder's long short story, *The Bridge of San Luis Rey*. In this book, he asks whether it was just by chance that those five people happened to be on the bridge in Peru that snapped in 1715, or was there some connection which brought them together at that moment. It turned out that the life of each one of those persons was being directed by someone in Lima. The book is really a parable of divine providence. One might say that it was by chance that St Matthias rather than Joseph called Barsabbas was elected to be an apostle, as he was chosen by lot; but it was clearly part of God's plan that he was chosen in this way (*Ac* 1:26).

3. Providence and Necessity

Our third objection is the opposite of the second. Instead of saying that the world cannot be ruled by divine providence because many things happen by chance, this objection holds that God does not rule the world by his providence because many things are necessitated or determined. When we say that providence is certain and infallible, this does not mean that God's plan imposes necessity on us, because his plan is known only to himself and thus we still act freely. The ways of providence can only be partially discerned in this life: they will only be fully known at the end.

Many people are unprepared to commit themselves to upholding free will. This may be because they think that the material world either moves by chance or that it is determined. Both these things are opposed to free will, because in neither way are we able to control our actions. We can see, however, that the world is not necessitated, because many events are thought to be contingent: that is, they might not have happened. Without laws of nature, which set the parameters, so to speak, for the movement of material bodies, there would be no order in the universe, as there manifestly is. Equally, there would be no order if everything happened by chance.

Belief in alternative higher forces

A sign that many think that we do not act freely but are subject to higher forces of nature is the rapid rise in the popularity of astrology in the last few decades. Astrology was popular in the Middle Ages and is so again today. Astrologists claim to be able to explain personality and to predict the course of people's lives by the conjunction of the stars and planets. There is a certain truth in astrology, because the disposition of our body could be influenced by the heavenly bodies, as one body can act on another. And our bodily disposition may partly explain some of our choices. Dispositions, however, are only dispositions: they do not determine our will, so that we could not have acted otherwise.[17] A person with a given disposition or personality is still free to choose one way or another. God alone rules our lives, not the stars. Trust in astrology is incompatible with belief in divine providence: it is a form of superstition.

In one of his Father Brown stories, *The Doom of the Darnaways*, G.K. Chesterton shows that although someone in the family seems to be 'fated' to be murdered in each generation, no one is fated to be murdered because murder is always due to someone's free choice. When people lose their hold on a right belief about God, they may well resort to invoking fate as the cause of many events in our lives. Belief in fate is, like astrology, incompatible with belief in divine providence, if by fate you mean that everything is determined by forces of nature. Boethius, however, later followed in this by St Thomas Aquinas, thought that fate had a place within providence, for the reason that God's plan is partly executed by the natural order: for example, by storms, floods, earthquakes or lack of rain with resulting poor harvests.[18] One has only to recall that the Hebrews were originally led down into Egypt because of a famine in Canaan.

It is significant that the ancients, who widely believed in fate, did not think that the three Fates: Clotho, Lachesis and Atropos, could be moved by prayer. Obviously, if everything were ruled by fate, there would be no point in praying to God for things, since they would already be determined. Thus praying to God for things rests on belief in divine providence. A fatalist thinks that there is no point in praying because I can make no difference to what will happen either way, for good or bad; so I may as well resign myself to what is bound to happen. Fatalism clearly shows a lack of hope. We shall see in the next section that prayer can make a difference to what happens in providence.

Petitionary Prayer

We cannot understand petitionary prayer apart from divine providence. We pray to God because we think that our prayer will make a difference to the course of events: for example, someone will be restored to health, pass an exam, be successful in an interview and so obtain work, find a nice friend or have a safe journey, because we and others have prayed for these things. It only makes sense to pray to God about things which come within his providence: there would be no use in turning to God in matters which lay outside his control.

To pray to anyone other than God is superstition or idolatry and shows a lack of trust, and so of hope, in God. When people do not put their hope in God, they put their hope in something else, which is idolatry. It is wrong to consult mediums and call up the spirits of the dead because it is to make a pact with demons and to try to find out something we are not meant to know. King Saul asked the witch of Endor to call up the spirit of Samuel because he lacked trust in God (*1 S* 28:6). We ought to be taught by God rather than evil spirits, and should not consult spirits, because God alone is omniscient.[19] When Catholics pray to the saints, whose power of intercession is greater than of those on earth, they do not pray to someone else than God but only ask the saints to pray to God on their behalf.

Nevertheless, even when it has been shown that all things fall within divine providence, someone might still ask, what is the purpose of praying for things to happen one way rather than another when providence is certain? And what difference can prayer make when God's will has been set from eternity and is immutable? It is well to be clear that we do not pray to change God's mind. Nor do we pray to let God know what we want, for he already knows this: as Jesus himself said in the Sermon on the Mount, "Your heavenly Father knows that you need all these things" (*Mt* 6:32). So why do we pray to God for things when his mind is not changed by our prayers? And how can he be said to hear our prayers unless he is moved by them?

Prayer in the Scriptures

First, we pray for things to happen in a certain way because not everything in providence is necessary. Part of God's providence is that he has given some creatures free will and thus he wills many things to be brought about in providence by their free choices. Second, we pray for things which are not yet fixed in their causes: for example, that some hostages will be freed but not that an eclipse of the sun or moon be deferred. Third, we pray because prayer is a part of God's plan of providence, as it is his will that we pray things.

Thus we pray for things because it is God's will that we do so. Jesus taught us that we "ought always to pray" (*Lk* 18:1). Likewise, St Paul exhorted the Thessalonians to "pray constantly, giving thanks in all circumstances; for this is the will of God in Christ Jesus for you" (*1 Th* 5:17-18). He also said, "let your requests be made known to God" (*Ph* 4:6).

Prayer is a part of God's plan of providence, because it *causes* things to come about: for example, the recovery of an ill person. How is this? Prayer plays a role in providence, although it does not change God's will, because he wills some good things for people who he knows from eternity will pray for them. Prayer is a cause of things happening in providence because it is done by agents with free will, who through their free choices bring about many things in providence. To pray is itself an act of free will. We cause things by our actions and prayer is an activity. So it is not surprising that it causes things when we reflect that prayer is quite a large part of the daily activity of some people, who may spend two or three hours, or even more, of each day in prayer. Although prayer does not change God's eternal will, it is effective, because it is part of God's providence that many things in it should be asked for in prayer.

What should we pray for?

What should we pray for? St Paul tells Timothy that we should pray for godliness and contentment, and food and clothing (*1 Tm* 6:6-8). In other words, for things which contribute to our spiritual good and for the necessities of life. In the 'Our Father' we pray, "Give us this day our daily bread", for we depend on providence that there is always enough bread for us every day. But sometimes we do not know how to pray or what we ought to pray for. Then, St Paul says, "we do not know how to pray, but the Spirit intercedes for us" (*Rm* 8:26). The Spirit does not literally pray, because God does not pray; but the Spirit helps us to pray according to the will of God. When Christ is said to intercede for us before the Father, this is not as he is God but as he is man, because he is our great High Priest (*Heb* 7:25). It is perhaps in this way that we can understand Christ's promise to grant whatever we ask for: "Whatever you ask for in my name, I will do it, that the Father may be glorified in the Son" (*Jn* 14:13). We are granted things when we ask for what is according to God's will. We also see here another reason why we should pray for things although we do not change God's mind: because, when they have been prayed for, the granting of them lets God's glory be seen. Prayer cannot fail to be a cause of things coming about, because God moves us to pray for them in the first place. He first inspires us with the good desires that we express in our prayers. Likewise, the Holy Spirit inspires us by enabling us to pray according to God's will. The purpose of prayer is not to change God's plan but to *obtain* what he wills.

What if God Does Not Give Us the Answer We Expect?

But we sometimes, perhaps often, find that our prayers are not directly answered by God. Does this mean that God is indifferent to our prayers or that these prayers have been in vain when they remain unanswered? There are several ways of seeing that prayer is always useful even when it is not answered as we wanted.

1. It is God's will that we pray for things. We do not bend God's will by our prayers but arouse our own trust, which it is necessary for us to have in him, because all things depend on him, who is the First Cause of everything. Thus prayer gives us the courage and strength to overcome difficulties. We see that prayer makes a difference because it produces the strength of will that is required for overcoming illness and great adversity. People who were near to death and tempted to resign themselves and let go of life have grasped it again and recovered to lead a normal life by earnest prayer. When King Hezekiah was on the point of dying, he turned his

face to the wall and prayed to the Lord, and recovered (*Is* 38:1-5).

2. We need to pray, because this makes us realise that we depend on God. This produces humility in us, which is necessary for us to have in prayer. Thus prayer is an act of hope, because by prayer we show that we do not rely on our own strength but look to God for help. Our own strength is not sufficient; whatever power things have comes from God in the first place: "apart from me you can do nothing" (*Jn* 15:5). When we hope in God we also gain confidence in prayer. When commenting on the request "Give us this day our daily bread", the *Catechism* says that we ask for it with the confidence of children that works with the providence of the Father.[20] In other words, prayer is a part of providence. We can pray with confidence because we are children of God. To have confidence in God was the distinctive teaching of St Thérèse of Lisieux about prayer. St Paul teaches us confidence in prayer when he writes that God "by the power at work within us is able to do far more abundantly than all that we ask or think" (*Ep* 3:20).

3. Whenever we pray we exercise the supernatural virtues of faith, hope and charity. No activity can be a more valuable than this because these virtues unite us with God. Thus prayer unites us with God, even when it does not bring us what we ask for. We only find the

fountain of life, for which we thirst, in God: "For with thee is the fountain of life" (*Ps* 35 (36): 9). Faith is the foundation of prayer; hope carries prayer through; charity is its end. The Church prays that we be "fervent in faith, hope and charity" in the collect for the sixteenth Sunday of Ordinary Time, and for "an increase of faith, hope and charity" on the thirtieth Sunday.

With faith we believe God is present everywhere, that he holds all things in existence, watches over all things and guides them. Praying for things is founded on faith in God's almighty power.

Hope gives us the confidence to ask for things. It enables us to persevere in prayer, because with hope we keep our destination in view. By hope we persist in prayer, like the widow who did not give up asking the judge for justice (*Lk* 18:3-5). Hope is founded on God's love of us: "hope does not disappoint us, because God's love has been poured into our hearts through the Holy Spirit, who has been given to us" (*Rm* 5:5).

The end of prayer is that we grow in charity, that is, in the love of God and of others. We express our love for others by praying for them. Moreover, we are drawn to prayer in the first place by the love of God inspiring us to pray. Although we cannot love God without first having faith that he exists, charity is the root of all the virtues. St Paul prayed that we, "being rooted and grounded in love" may come to know with the saints the breadth and length and height and depth of the love of Christ (*Ep* 3:17-20). Thus unanswered prayer is never entirely fruitless, because at least we grow in charity, as prayer springs from the love of God and draws us more closely to him.

4. Prayer manifests our *desire* for what God wants to give, and may help to arouse or increase that desire. God wants us first to show our desire in prayer for two reasons. First, if we did not need to show our desire by praying for things, we might take them for granted as we have not needed much to ask for them. Second, if we did not need to pray for them, we might be less grateful having received them. Gratitude is a virtue, and St Paul often told his new converts to Christianity to pray with thanksgiving in all circumstances, as he gave thanks to God for their faith, hope and love (*1 Th* 1:2-3). Thus prayer expresses and raises our desire for heavenly gifts, the things which God most wants to give us. St Augustine, in his letter on prayer to Proba, tells her that we pray with insistent desire in faith, hope and charity, but also with words at certain hours to arouse and increase our desire. He adds that prayer can prevent us from becoming lukewarm in our faith by being preoccupied with the cares of this world.[21]

Although we do not change God's mind or let him know anything which he does not already know, by prayer we *dispose* ourselves better for what he has to give us, especially his gifts of grace. In the same letter to Proba, St Augustine tells her "he [God] wishes our desire to be put into practice in prayer" so that we may be able to receive what he, in his providence, has prepared to give us. These things even surpass anything we can imagine or think of: "'What no eye has seen, nor ear heard, nor the heart of man conceived, what God has prepared for those who love him', God has revealed to us through the Spirit" (*1 Co* 2:9-10). For the same reason, Christ told the apostles to return to Jerusalem after he had ascended to heaven and to wait for power from on high to come down on them before they went out to preach the Gospel to the whole world (*Lk* 24:49). We may suppose that in those nine days between the Ascension and Pentecost the apostles with Mary prepared themselves for the gift of the Holy Spirit by continual prayer.

Thus prayer helps us to realise that we depend on God, to desire his gifts more greatly, and to dispose ourselves better to receive them.

5. Even so, prayer often seems to be in vain when it is unanswered. Let us, then, suppose for a moment that God answered all our prayers. Prayer would then seem to work automatically: you would only have to pray for something and you would receive it. But God is not bound by our requests anymore than he is by the laws of nature (so miracles are always possible). If God granted

all our prayers immediately, he would seem to be bound by us rather than to rule creation freely. Also, if all our prayers were answered, we would not so easily recognise that when a prayer is granted it is through God's *grace*.

One reason why God does not always answer our prayer immediately is that he has something *better* in store for us than we thought of or because we ask for something which, with hindsight, we can see would not have been so good for us. This point was well understood by Shakespeare, who admirably expressed it thus:

> We, ignorant of ourselves,
> Beg often our own harms, which the wise powers
> Deny us for our good; so we find profit
> By losing our prayers.[22]

In this case God hears our prayer, although he does not seem to. The better wine was kept to the end at the marriage feast of Cana (*Jn* 2:10). We can reflect on this point in the second Mystery of Light of the Rosary.

6. Finally, prayer clearly helps men and women to follow the will of God and to live virtuously, by doing which they reach their blessed end, to live with God eternally in glory. Thus prayer furthers God's plan of providence as predestination is part of providence. Predestination itself is God's plan for those who are going to be saved by grace. God does not predestine people because they pray

but prayer helps them to obtain the grace for the virtues they need to reach the blessed end. Thus prayer does not cause predestination, which initially comes from God's grace, but furthers God's plan by helping people to achieve the means of living virtuously that leads to the end. Prayer helps us to obtain the virtues because we need grace for the virtues; otherwise we think we can rely on our own strength to be saved.

As we can see from the above six points, prayer is never pointless but brings us great benefits even when it appears to be unanswered. When we realise this, we will pray with greater hope and love. If we thought that prayer has little effect or none, we might think that there is no need to pray because either things are going to turn out well anyway, say, I am going to get better, or it is not God's providence that I get better and so nothing can change this. To think the first is presumption (I do not need to pray because good will be granted anyway); to think the second is fatalist (I can do nothing to avert evil). Both attitudes betray a lack of hope. By prayer we can draw good out of evil, like an unhappy situation or suffering, either for ourselves or for others. We pray because we have hope, and we hope because a miracle is always possible. Christians have hope of eternal life especially because of the greatest miracle of all: the resurrection of Jesus Christ from the dead by the Father.

Miracles

A miracle, strictly speaking, occurs when a natural effect is achieved without its natural cause: for example, when someone is suddenly cured of blindness, lameness, or some physical deformity, for no apparent reason. Cures at Lourdes are declared to be miracles when doctors from all over the world, including some without belief in God, after examining the medical evidence agree in declaring that there is 'no known cause' of the cure. Miracles are properly restricted to physical events and only to things which normally happen through natural causes if at all. Moral changes, like extraordinary conversions, do not count as miracles in the strict sense, because it is not possible to establish clear, objective criteria for them. Moral 'miracles' are more the work of grace than an inexplicable alteration of nature. It is necessary to have strict criteria for counting anything as a miracle, otherwise it is easy to cast doubt on the claim for a miracle and miracles would cease to impress.

The occurrence of miracles means that we do not live in a deterministic universe and thus that it is always worthwhile to pray for things, because God on occasions intervenes in the normal course of nature. If miracles were not possible, God would be constrained by nature and its laws. God has the power to work miracles because he created everything immediately, not through intermediary beings. Miracles manifest his power over creation and show him to be Lord of the universe: "Who is this that even the sea and winds obey him?" (*Mt* 8:27) Thus belief in miracles rests on a right understanding of the doctrine of creation. People generally suppose that miracles do not just happen by chance but have a cause: when they are not explicable by any natural cause, we ascribe them to a higher cause than nature, to the cause of all nature, God himself.

Against miracles

Many people find it difficult to believe in miracles or simply dismiss reports of them. Even Christians doubt many of the miracles in the Bible. But the Scottish atheist philosopher, David Hume (1711-1776) rightly saw that no one could consistently accept the Christian religion without also believing in miracles: the resurrection of Jesus Christ to start with. Christian faith rests on the Gospels and the miracle stories are inextricably part of these Gospels. Hume produced a famous set of arguments against belief in miracles, which can be read in chapter ten of his *Enquiry concerning Human Understanding*. Knowing them can help believers to counter the arguments of those who dismiss miracles.

Thus it will be useful to summarise a few of Hume's arguments here, because they are likely to recur in debate today. Hume first defined a miracle as a violation of the laws of nature and observed that the reports of miracles are based on the testimony of witnesses but the acceptance of testimony depends on the uniform experience of people, which he thought is our sole guide in matters of fact. As there can be no uniform experience of miracles because they are by definition exceptions to the common experience of nature and contrary to the laws of nature, we should prefer our experience of the laws of nature as more probable. Hume further argued that we have no reason to believe that events which have not been observed are similar to ones that have been observed and, therefore, we are not justified in taking anyone's experience of miracles as a reliable guide when we ourselves have no experience of them.

In favour of miracles

In his arguments against miracles, Hume betrays an unjustified and unduly pessimistic view of human nature, for he assumes that we cannot trust the report of any miracle since it is common for men to lie in any age. He doubts the integrity, good sense and motives of believers who spread the reports of miracles, which he thought were often to deceive people. Hume allows himself more easily to be persuaded by experience of the bad will of many people than by examples of veracity and honest motives; he trusted humanity too little. Just because some paintings that are put on the market turn out to be fakes does not mean that none are genuine.

Hume noted that we can only know about the attributes of God from experience of the effects he has produced in nature: his wisdom and power, and so on. But as miracles are contrary to nature, we cannot tell that they come from him. He forgot that, as God is the author of the laws of nature, he has the power at times to override them. Hume also suggested that, as events which only occur rarely are not likely to have a good reason, but God would only work a miracle for a good purpose, miracles are not probable. One can reply here that, on the contrary, it is because God works miracles for a good reason that they are rare; if they were common occurrences they might seem to be trivial and would certainly be less impressive.

Having seen the weaknesses in Hume's arguments against miracles and fairly met them, we may reasonably trust the testimony of miracles that has been well-established. Miracles are a sign that God has power over nature and thus governs it with his providence. Thus they assure our faith in his power, which is the foundation of praying to God for things, whether it be for the cure of an illness or good weather for a crossing of the sea.

What We Should Specially Pray For

It is right that we should pray for what we and others need in this life. These are our temporal needs. It is charity to pray for others. But we should not forget to pray for the things that we need most of all, that is, for what brings us everlasting good. Thus St Thomas Aquinas says that what we ought specially to pray for is the things which lead us to *beatitude* and so to lasting happiness in heaven.[23] The way that leads us to beatitude includes the things that make us better, which are not necessarily the things that make us happier as most people count happiness in this life. This is the point of the eight beatitudes in the Sermon on the Mount (*Mt* 5:3-12), that one can be truly blessed though not happy or fortunate in the common sense in the present life but rather poor and unjustly wronged. Aquinas says that we ought to pray for the effects of grace for ourselves and for others, for this is to pray for our spiritual good, which is a higher good. This is entirely in keeping with Our Lord's reminder that in asking for our daily bread we should not overlook to ask for the gift of the Holy Spirit: "If you then, who are evil, know how to give good gifts to your children, how much more will your heavenly Father give the Holy Spirit to those who ask him" (*Lk* 11:13). It is only charity to pray for our own true good as we pray for the needs of others, for the second commandment of charity is to love others as we love ourselves. We love ourselves by seeking our true good, the good that leads us to heaven. Thus prayer is founded on faith, is carried by hope, and ends in charity.

Endnotes

[1] *CCC* 304.
[2] Xenophon, *Memorabilia*, I 4.6.
[3] *The Consolation of Philosophy*, IV 6 (trans. Penguim Classics).
[4] *Summa Theologiae* (henceforth abbreviated as *ST*) 1a 22,1.
[5] Ibid., 1a 103, 1 ad 1.
[6] Ibid., 1a 103, 1.
[7] *CCC* 308.
[8] *CCC* 307.
[9] *Hamlet*, Act 5 sc.1.
[10] *Metaphysics*, Bk 3, c.4.
[11] *CCC* 310.
[12] *Chance or Purpose?*, 49.
[13] *CCC* 311.
[14] *ST* 1a 22, 2 ad 1.
[15] *The Consolation of Philosophy*, Bk 2, 8.
[16] *Physics*, Bk 2 c. 8.
[17] See Thomas Aquinas, *ST* 1a 115, 4.
[18] Boethius, *The Consolation of Philosophy*, Bk 4, 6.
[19] See Thomas Aquinas, *ST* 2a 2ae 92, 2.
[20] *CCC* 2830.
[21] Letter 130.
[22] *Anthony and Cleopatra*, Act 2 scene 1.
[23] *ST* 2a 2ae 83, 4 ad 5.

Prayer in the Family

John and Beth Viatori

For many children, the experience of prayer in the family shapes their attitude to prayer and their faith for the rest of their lives. For parents, insecurity with their own prayer life and the practical problems posed by small children or teenagers can make the practice of prayer at home seem impossible. This booklet gives practical advice on how the home can become an authentic school of prayer.

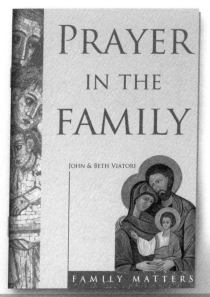

PA5   ISBN 978 1 86082 390 9

Deepening Prayer

Sr Mary David Totah OSB

Prayer is at the heart of the Christian life, but is always a battle. This booklet explores the opportunities of some of the main methods of Christian prayer, as well as the problems and pitfalls. Sr Mary David uses the wisdom of the Church Fathers to lead the reader into a deeper relationship with God.

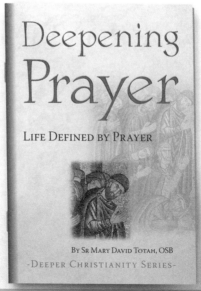

SP13   ISBN 978 1 86082 382 4

Conversational Prayer

Br Craig Driscoll

Conversational prayer brings us closer to Jesus: it's a friendship form of prayer - it can be done while 'on the go', that is, while working, travelling, shopping, and so forth. Throughout this booklet conversational prayer is written about as a conversation with Jesus - and also with our Father, with the Holy Spirit, with Our Lady, Saint Joseph, the other Saints and your Guardian Angel. Perhaps you too will start, if you haven't already, to engage in conversational prayer.

Conversational Prayer

A constant friendship with Jesus

D728   ISBN 978 1 86082 665 8